EARTH

Written by Alex Hall

ELEMENTS

Gareth Stevens
PUBLISHING

Please visit our website, www.garethstevens.com. For a free color catalog of all our high-quality books, call toll free 1-800-542-2595 or fax 1-877-542-2596.

Published in 2025 by
Gareth Stevens Publishing
2544 Clinton St.
Buffalo, NY 14224

Written by:
Alex Hall

Edited by:
Rebecca Phillips-Bartlett

Designed by:
Ker Ker Lee

Cataloging-in-Publication Data

Names: Hall, Alex.
Title: Earth / Alex Hall.
Description: Buffalo, NY : Gareth Stevens Publishing, 2025. | Series: Elements | Includes glossary and index.
Identifiers: ISBN 9781482468540 (pbk.) | ISBN 9781482468557 (library bound) | ISBN 9781482468564 (ebook)
Subjects: LCSH: Geology--Juvenile literature. | Four elements (Philosophy)--Juvenile literature. | Earth (Planet)--Juvenile literature.
Classification: LCC QE29.H355 2025 | DDC 551--dc23

This edition is published by arrangement with Booklife Publishing

Printed in the United States of America

CPSIA compliance information: Batch #CW25GS: For further information contact Gareth Stevens at 1-800-542-2595.

Find us on

Photo Credits – Images are courtesy of Shutterstock.com, with thanks to Getty Images, Thinkstock Photo, and iStockphoto.

Recurring images – gravity_point.
Cover – Ivaylo Ivanov, Valentina Shilkina, MD_style.
2–3 – NOPPHARAT88. 4–5 – Aphelleon, Radiokafka, Triff.
6–7 – Food Impressions, logoboom, New Africa, Nonchanon.
8–9 – Kolonko, Naeblys. 10–11 – fotohunter, Paul Maguire.
12–13 – Andrei Metelev, Jurgens Potgieter, Paul Maguire.
14–15 –Julian Frees, R R. 16–17 – Dzm1try, New Africa.
18–19 – Ground Picture, MOHAMED ABDULRAHEEM.
20–21 – Maria Symchych, Pavel L Photo and Video.
22–23 – Allison Jehlicka, lovelyday12.

CONTENTS

Words that look like <u>this</u> can be found in the glossary on page 24.

ESSENTIAL ELEMENTS

Life on our planet would not be possible without the four elements. The elements are water, earth, fire, and air. Each element has its own important job. Together, these elements keep the world in balance.

These elements are essential because the world cannot work without them.

The planet we live on is called Earth. It has the same name as the element called earth. This is because the ground you feel beneath your feet is made up of the earth element.

the earth element

the planet Earth

These facts about earth will rock your world!

WHAT IS EARTH?

The earth element is a solid. Solids are firm and do not change shape easily. Rocks, soil, and sand are all part of this element. They are often found when someone digs into the ground.

Rocks, soil, and sand are made of minerals. The minerals have been put together in different ways. This is why rocks are hard but soil and sand feel soft.

LAYERS OF EARTH

Planet Earth is made up of different layers. The top layer is called the crust. This layer is made of earth. Plants grow from this layer.

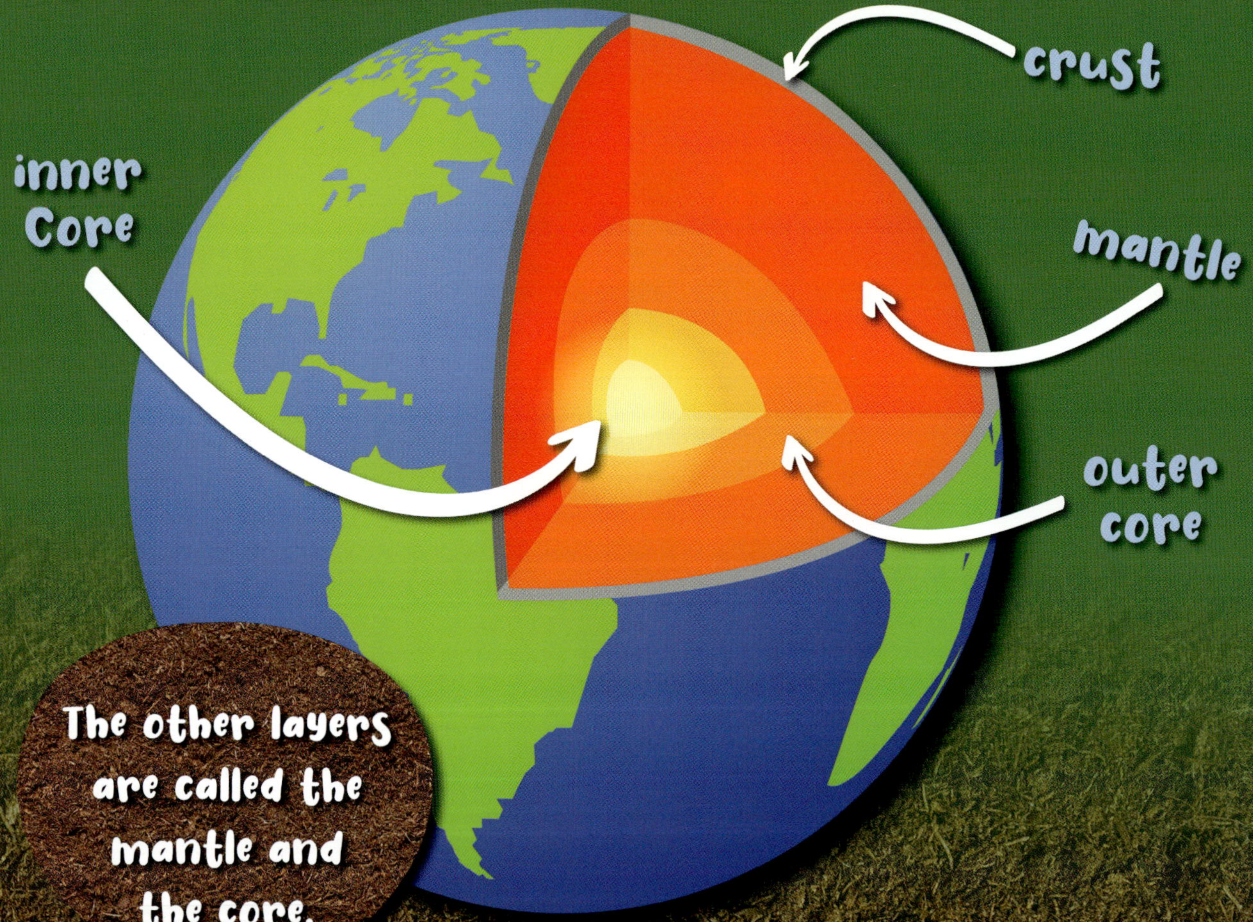

The other layers are called the mantle and the core.

Planet Earth's crust is made up of large pieces of rock called tectonic plates. Tectonic plates are always slowly moving underground.

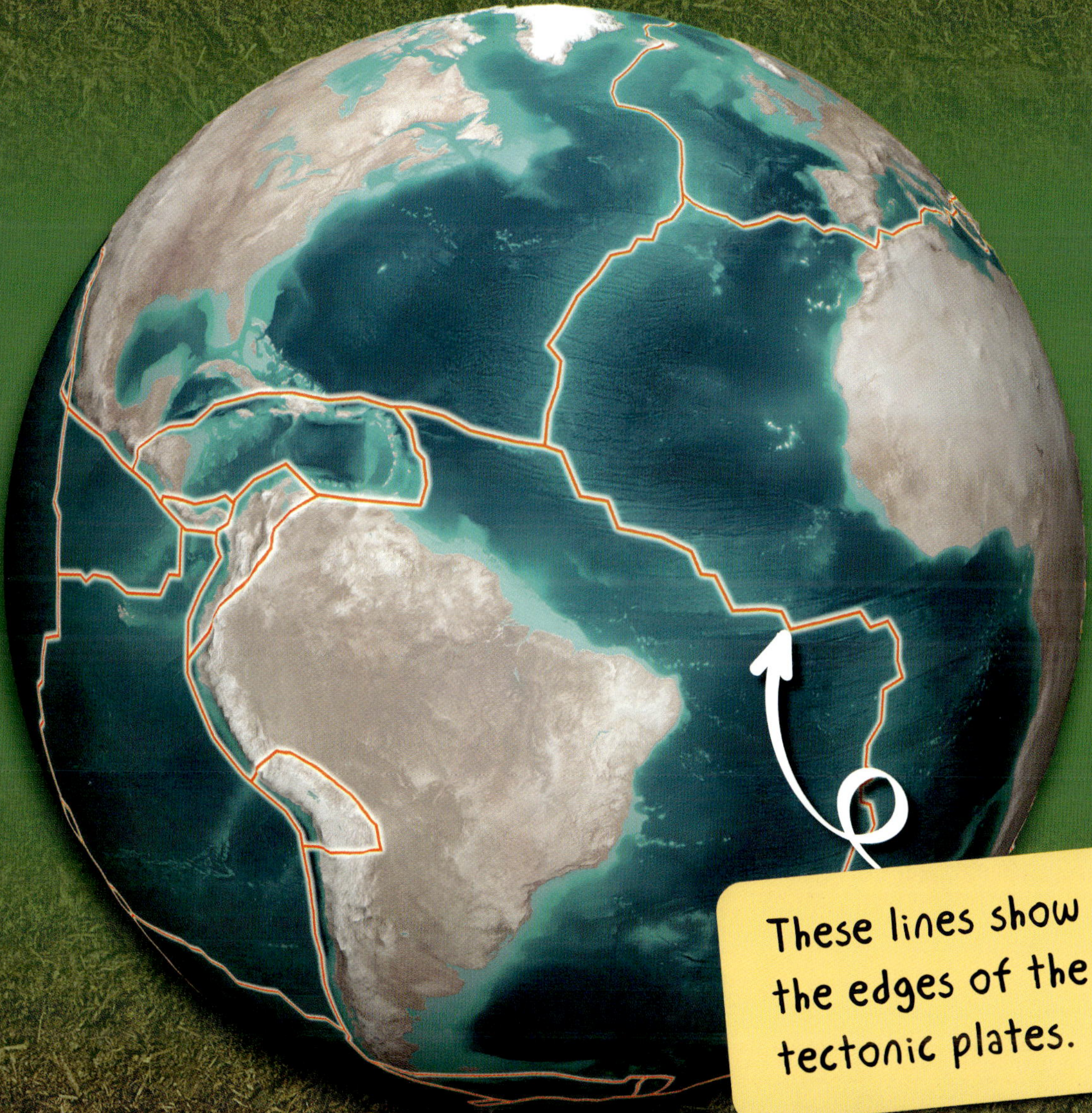

These lines show the edges of the tectonic plates.

THE ROOT OF LIFE

Earth is a very important element. It gives life to many living things. Most soil is full of nutrients. Plants use these nutrients to grow. Humans then use these plants to grow food.

Plants make a gas called oxygen. Humans and animals breathe oxygen. Since plants need earth to grow, and we need plants to make the oxygen we breathe, we could not live without earth.

We could not live without the food and oxygen plants make.

A WORLD UNDER YOUR FEET

The soil is home to many animals. Animals such as moles, badgers, rabbits, and worms live in underground habitats. A habitat is the place an animal or plant lives.

rabbit

earthworm

Some animals use the earth for different things. Many elephants dig holes in the earth to find water underground. Elephants sometimes use the mud they dig from the earth to protect themselves from sunburn.

EARTHQUAKES

Earthquakes are natural disasters. Natural disasters are events caused by nature and not by humans. Sometimes, Earth's tectonic plates move suddenly and make the ground shake. This is called an earthquake.

Some earthquakes are more dangerous than others. Sometimes, earthquakes are so small that people barely notice them. Stronger earthquakes can shake buildings until they fall down.

Earthquakes can destroy, or cause great harm, to whole cities!

STAYING SAFE

Earthquakes can be dangerous. Earthquakes remind us how powerful the elements can be. Although strong earthquakes are rare, or uncommon, it is still important to know how to stay safe if an earthquake happens.

WHAT TO DO IF AN EARTHQUAKE HITS:

- Drop to the ground to avoid being knocked over.
- Duck under a strong desk or table, or cover your neck and head with your arms and hands.
- Hold on to your shelter.

If you are outside, stay away from buildings or anything that could fall.

SOIL POLLUTION

Soil pollution is what happens when harmful matter is put into the earth. Most soil pollution comes from the garbage we throw away in landfills. Landfills often make the soil underneath them too polluted to grow anything in.

Landfills are piles of human garbage that have been collected.

Soil pollution is bad for the environment. Pollution stops plants from growing in the area, which means animals run out of food. Recycling can help reduce, or lessen, landfill waste and stop pollution.

SHAPING THE EARTH

Many minerals found in earth can be used to make building materials. Bricks are made of something called clay that is found under the ground. Cement is made of sand.

Some building materials are made from earth.

Earth is used for fun things too. Wet clay is easy to shape. When something made of clay dries, it is called pottery. What would you make with clay?

EXCITING EARTH

The element of earth is so important to life on our planet. It provides what plants need to grow so they can give off oxygen. Earth is also home to many amazing animals.

Earth is an incredible element in so many ways. Earth is in the walls of your home and the ground you walk on. What else can you think of that uses earth?

GLOSSARY

balance the state in which things exist in the correct amounts to keep things stable

environment the natural world

gas matter that spreads out to fill any space available

material matter from which something is made

mineral matter in the ground that forms rocks

nutrient something a living thing needs to stay alive

recycling using something again to make something else

INDEX